ARE YOU A PUZZLE MASTER?

Can you solve the mysteries of Ghostly Mansion?
Why is it empty and silent during the day?
What frightening creatures fill it at night?
What unsolved puzzles and strange secrets lurk
behind its heavy wooden door?
No one knows.
No one has dared go near...until now.
Join Matt, Susan, Tom, and their dog Patches as
they explore this mysterious mansion. Help them
solve its puzzles and discover its secrets.
They're not afraid...are you?

A Reader's Digest Kids Book
Published by The Reader's Digest Association, Inc.
Produced by Joshua Morris Publishing, Inc.
Copyright © 1991 John Speirs
With additional text by Gill Speirs
Library of Congress Cataloging in Publication Data
Speirs, John.
Ghostly Games / conceived and illustrated by John Speirs.
p. cm.
"Puzzle masters."
ISBN 0-89577-393-7
1. Picture puzzles. 2. Maze puzzles. I. Title.
GV1507. P47S67 1991
793.73–dc20
91-22407
CIP
AC
READER'S DIGEST and the Pegasus logo are registered trademarks of The Reader's Digest Association, Inc.
Printed in Singapore

John Speirs

PUZZLE MASTERS

Ghostly Games

Reader's Digest Kids
PLEASANTVILLE, N.Y. – MONTREAL

MONSTER MAZE

Dense, sinister hedges form a maze blocking the entrance to Ghostly Mansion. The sun sets. Though the evening is windless, the leaves of the hedges begin to whisper. Spooky shadows flit past.

"What lives in these hedges?" wonders Tom.

"We'll have to find our way through them," says Matt, "if we want to explore Ghostly Mansion."

"Let's split up," suggests Susan. "Matt and Tom, you go together. Patches and I will try another way."

"Let's try to get there without running into anybody ... or anything!" says Tom.

Find the only path you can take to Ghostly Mansion without bumping into any spooks, creeps, or monsters. Go another way, following the letters in the right order to learn a secret message.

WHO'S WATCHING?

A rotting stair groans underfoot as the explorers reach the front door of Ghostly Mansion.

With both hands, Matt lifts the huge brass knocker and lets it fall against the door.

"There's no one here," says Tom.

"Shh! Listen!" cries Susan, her ear to the door. "What is that shuffling sound?"

With a creak, the door grinds open. They see a huge man with smoldering red eyes and a monocle.

"I am Igor," he says, his voice hollow and sad. "Welcome to Ghostly Mansion."

He reaches out a long, quivering arm to pat Patches with a flat, bony hand. To escape Igor's creepy touch, Patches slips away and rushes into the house.

With slow, dragging steps, Igor turns around. He beckons for the others to follow him. "Come in," he says. "The keys are the key."

They look at each other. What does he mean? Do they dare go inside?

"No turning back now," says Susan. "Anyway, we've got to find Patches."

Wide-eyed, the children inch forward into the gathering gloom.

To find Patches, the explorers will probably need the flashlight, magnifying glass, and candle that are hidden in this picture. Can you find them all? Where is Patches? And what was that about a key?

POLTERGEIST PICTURES

The children make their way across a creepy, bat-tiled floor into the picture gallery. Row upon row of dusty paintings line the walls. A musty monster lurking in the corner shrieks with laughter.

"They think they're so spooky," chuckles Susan.

Matt studies a huge painting. "This is strange," he says. "This picture was painted in 1760. But look at the sky! They didn't have jet planes then."

"The paint is still wet," says Susan.

"Poltergeists!" says Tom. "They're changing things all over the painting. I wonder if Igor knows about this?"

"Where is he, anyway?" asks Susan, looking around.

Can you find twenty things in the painting that don't belong there and must have been added by the poltergeists? It seems like Igor has been around. Do you see his signature?

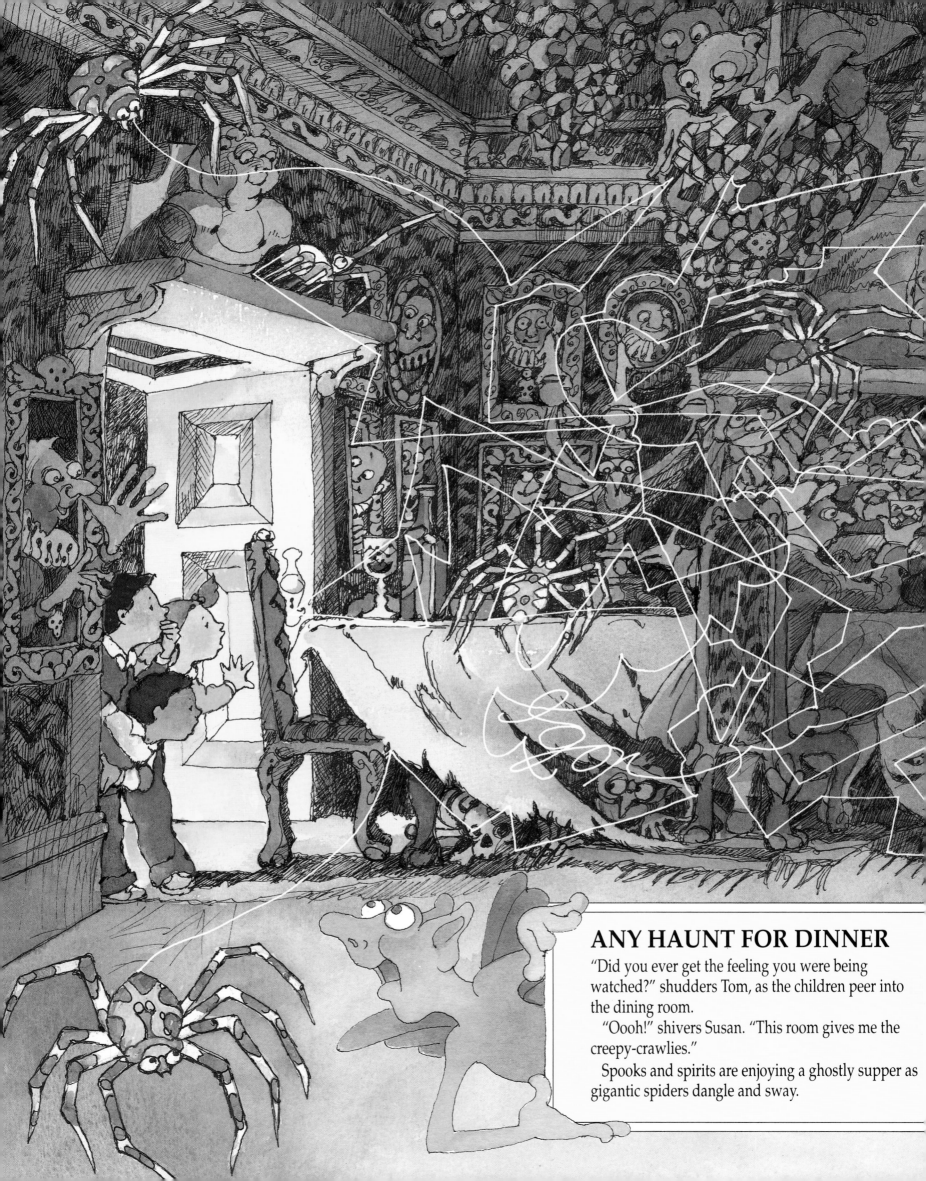

ANY HAUNT FOR DINNER

"Did you ever get the feeling you were being watched?" shudders Tom, as the children peer into the dining room.

"Oooh!" shivers Susan. "This room gives me the creepy-crawlies."

Spooks and spirits are enjoying a ghostly supper as gigantic spiders dangle and sway.

They turn to go, but are stopped by a howl from Patches.

"He's stuck in a spider's web!" says Susan. "We've got to rescue him!"

Which spider has Patches trapped in its sticky web? Igor may not be in the room, but a spider has spun his name. Can you find which spider did it?

THINGS THAT GO AAAGH! IN THE NIGHT

"Are you sure we should keep exploring this house?" asks Tom as they trudge up the stairs.

Susan glances at him. "Scared?"

"Er, no," shrugs Tom. "Just asking…"

Dragging chains clank and grind just behind them.

"Something is following us!" shrieks Tom.

Matt throws open a door. "Quick! In here!" he says. The others race after him.

They are in a musty, dank bedroom. Tom bumps into a bed. A cloud of dust rises. For a moment, they are surrounded by silence.

Then, they hear eerie sounds that are hard to place. Fluttering wings – do they belong to a vampire bat? Something's dripping – is it a leaky water faucet or the spattering of slime? What is that ticking – a clock or the heart of a ghost? What is whining – a mosquito, a mouse, or a singing spook? Is the clicking a cricket, a beetle, or the scratching fingertips of a bodyless hand?

Can you find all the things that could have made those scary sounds? Are the children still going the right way? To find out, see if Igor is around.

SEEING DOUBLE

With a hard push against a heavy trapdoor, the explorers land in the attic of Ghostly Mansion. A breeze swishes the curtains. Creatures of the night swoop and swirl around the clutter that is piled to the ceiling.

"Look out! A vampire bat!" says Tom, ducking to avoid the flash of wings.

"Am I seeing double or is everything happening twice?" wonders Susan, rubbing her eyes.

One side of the picture looks like a mirror image of the other – except for fourteen differences, including a special message from Igor. Spot the differences, and figure out what Igor's message says.

SPOOKY PICTURES

Igor leads the explorers back down the stairs.

"Look at these strange paintings!" says Matt. "Why would anyone want to paint dead trees … or this strange woman?"

"I don't see that," says Tom.

Some of these paintings look like two different things – what do you see when you look at them?

"Those skulls are all smiling," says Susan.

"*All* smiling?" whispers Igor.

The children jump as a whining sound rushes up the stairs. "That would be the four Howlies," nods Igor. "They're locked under the floor. They're identical."

Igor is wrong about the Howlies – they're not identical. Can you find the two that are different? For that matter, one of the skulls in the picture Susan is looking at is different from all the others, too. Can you find it?

EEE-EEEK!

"Mice!" squeal the children.

"There must be hundreds of them!" shouts Matt, amazed.

Pots and pans and cups and saucers rattle and shake in the Ghostly Mansion kitchen as the mice run riot.

"That ghost's hair is full of mice," whispers Tom, pointing at a chubby spook.

"They're all over the food, too," says Susan, wrinkling her nose.

"Igor! How can you put up with this?" wonders Matt, looking around. Igor was nowhere in sight.

"Where's Patches?" said Tom. "I can hear him, but I can't see him anywhere."

The children walk around on tiptoes, trying to find Patches without stepping on any mice.

Where is Patches? Can you find the two mice that are identical? Can you find the two white mice? Igor is watching again. Where is he?

INTO THE JAWS OF THE DUNGEON

Matt, Susan, and Tom squeeze after Patches through a rusty iron door. It slams shut behind them. As their eyes slowly get used to the dim light, they realize …

"We're locked in a dungeon!" shouts Tom.

"Watch out! The steps are covered with slippery slime!" cries Susan.

A ghoul flutters past. "Those ghosts will trip us up if they can," says Matt.

"I hope not !" says Susan. "Have you seen what's down there?"

In the churning water below, crocodiles thrash, their greedy jaws opening wide and snapping shut hungrily.

"We've got to get out of here!" says Tom.

"Over here!" Igor's hollow voice rings out. "A key to the door lies over here. But you'll need the other seven keys, too!"

The explorers need your help. Find the other seven keys. They are hidden in the mansion. Trace a safe path through the white or yellow water to the eighth key. Don't run into any crocodiles! Trace another path from there to the steps that lead to the door with eight locks. Igor seems to be enjoying this – where is he?

TIME'S ALMOST OUT

The shrill ring of an alarm clock shatters the air. A moment of silence follows, then chaos. The children are almost knocked off their feet as ghosts rush past them from every direction, pushing them along in their frantic flight.

"Matt! Tom!" calls Susan. "Where are you?"

"Here!" cries Matt from one direction.

"Over here!" calls Tom from another.

As the ghosts fly past, they grasp at the children, hissing "The keys … the keys … we must have the keys!"

"What's happening?" asks Susan as she's spun around by a racing ghoul. "What time is it?"

Tom squints at his watch, which glows faintly in the half-light. "It's 5:55 A.M.," he says.

Can you find Tom, Susan, Matt, Igor, and Patches among the terrified freaks? Where are the eight keys the ghosts are trying to snatch? Can you find the alarm clock?

TIME HAS RUN OUT
YOU HAVE BEEN WARNED
THIS ANCIENT MESSAGE
MUST NOT BE SCORNED
ALL DREADED CREATURES
OF THE NIGHT
MUST HIDE AWAY

CRYPTIC MAZE

Igor tries to slip away, but this time the children are too fast for him. They follow him into the cellar of Ghostly Mansion.

Some tardy specters lurk around shadowy coffins. Bats flutter frantically.

"Look!" says Susan, pointing to a rhyme on the cellar wall. The children rush to read it.

"Some words are missing!" cries Tom.

Igor has left a final puzzle – a poem with some missing words! The letters to form them are hidden throughout the house. If you take the right path while leaving the house, you'll find the letters you need. You'll also find out why the ghosts were so panicked. But after you find out, please don't tell anybody. Igor would be most disappointed to find out that you had revealed the secret of Ghostly Mansion.

GHOSTLY ANSWERS

Monster Maze

No spooks, creeps, or monsters will bother you along the path traced with a BLUE line. By following the path traced with a RED line, you'll run into some scary creatures. But you'll also pick up the letters that spell this secret message: FIND ALL THE KEYS.

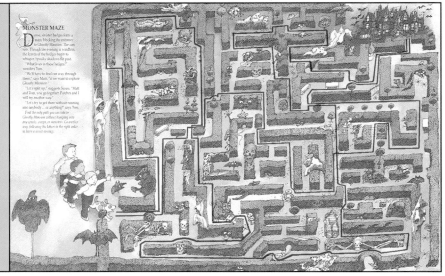

Who's Watching?

The candle, magnifying glass, and flashlight are circled in RED. Patches is circled in BLUE. The first of eight keys is shown in BLUE. And you'll find one in each of the next seven scenes.

Poltergeist Pictures

Circled in RED are all the things the poltergeists must have painted. They are a motorboat with water-skier, jet airplane, ski lift, telescope and observatory, soda can and straw, telephone poles and wires, cowboy hat, "happy face" button, portable radio with headphones, fountain pen, book with crossword puzzle, Eiffel Tower bookmark, wristwatch, zippered belt pouch, sneaker, telescopic sight on gun, tennis ball, dog collar and license, modern house, bicycle, satellite dish on roof, tractor, and TV antenna. Did you find at least 20? Igor's signature is circled in BLUE.

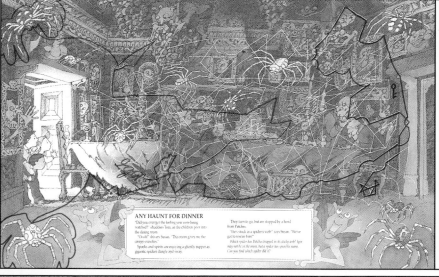

Any Haunt for Dinner

The spider circled in RED has trapped Patches in its sticky web under a chair. The spider circled in BLUE has spun Igor's name.

Things That Go Aaagh! in the Night

All the things and creatures that could have made those scary sounds are circled in RED. Igor is circled in BLUE.

Seeing Double

All 14 differences, including Igor's message are circled in RED. If you hold up Igor's message on the right to a mirror, it will read FOLLOW ME.

Spooky Pictures

The skull that is different in the picture is circled in BLUE.
The other six pictures contain these two images:
1. Three bare trees and the figure of Igor.
2. A lady wearing hair ornaments and the face of a rat.
3. An island and two sleeping dogs.
4. A large skull and a lady looking in the mirror of a dressing table.
5. A young lady facing away and an old lady wearing a monocle.
6. A candle and two ghouls.

The differences among the "Howlies"
are circled in RED.

Eee-Eeek!

Igor and Patches are circled in RED. The two identical mice and the two white mice are circled in BLUE.

Into the Jaws of the Dungeon

The eighth and final key is shown here in BLUE.
The waterway traced with a BLUE line is the one safe path to the eighth key.
The waterway traced with a RED line leads the way out.
Igor is circled in RED.

Time's Almost Out

Tom, Susan, Matt, Patches, and Igor are circled in RED.
The eight keys are shown in BLUE.
The alarm clock is circled in BLUE.

Cryptic Maze

If you follow the RED line through the rooms of the mansion, you'll pick up the letters that read AT FIRST SUNLIGHT. All the ghouls and ghosts must be back in their resting places before daybreak, otherwise they will vanish forever. That is the final secret of Ghostly Mansion ... but don't tell anyone!

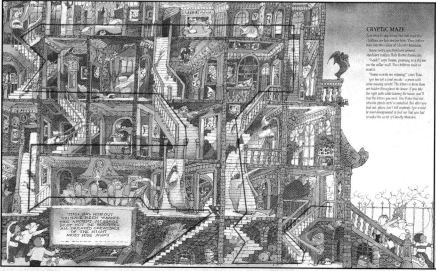